When

poems by

Elaine Nadal

Finishing Line Press
Georgetown, Kentucky

When

Copyright © 2020 by Elaine Nadal
ISBN 978-1-64662-146-0 First Edition
All rights reserved under International and Pan-American Copyright Conventions. No part of this book may be reproduced in any manner whatsoever without written permission from the publisher, except in the case of brief quotations embodied in critical articles and reviews.

ACKNOWLEDGMENTS

These poems have appeared in the following journals/anthologies:

"A Dream" (*Rigorous Magazine*)
"BEYOND" and "Beyond" (*The Write Launch*)
"Frescavena y Morir Soñando" (*Pilgrimage Magazine*)
"Remains" (*The Americas Poetry Festival of New York 2018 Anthology*)
"The Question" (*HOOT Review*)
"To The Saxophone Abuela Bought For My Aunt
Who Later Passed It On To My Mother,
Who Handed It to Me" (*Latino Book Review Magazine*)

Many thanks to my husband Frederick Hashemian for his support, encouragement, and feedback.

Publisher: Leah Maines
Editor: Christen Kincaid
Guest Editor: Frederick Hashemian
Cover Art: Jasleni Brito
Author Photo: Frederick Hashemian
Cover Design: Jasleni Brito

Printed in the USA on acid-free paper.
Order online: www.finishinglinepress.com
also available on amazon.com

Author inquiries and mail orders:
Finishing Line Press
P. O. Box 1626
Georgetown, Kentucky 40324
U. S. A.

Table of Contents

When 1
The House 2
Name 3
Beyond 4
Cindy 5
Michelle's Secret 6
Remains 7
To the Saxophone Abuela Bought For My Aunt
    Who Later Passed It On To My Mother,
    Who Handed It to Me 8
Fear 10
Mind-full 11
A Dream 12
The Question 13
The Door 14
Guilt 15
Iker 16
Daughter 17
Sorry 19
Frescavena y Morir Soñando 20
Liberation 22
Speak 23
Stay Silent 24
Accent 25
Omnipresent: An Ode to My Accent 26
Duende 27
Hope 28
Vidal 29
Beyond Perspective 30
Perspectives 31
BEYOND 32

When

When the sky is pink, lavender, and celestial blue,
when the clouds are notes or fragments of songs,
I try to read them like a medicine woman
though I possess no magic. I attempt to
interpret them like a chronicler despite
my inability to explain my genealogy
or the curses brought to my house.

The House

There's a heat in our house that covers and asphyxiates.
It feels heavy when he's around.
The stones are my support.
They bear the lessons and punishments.
He feeds me, but so much bread is stifling,
and in his absence, I'm on a fast.
I don't know what to do with myself.
I change the curtains;
I wash the pillows and arrange them.
My body spills salt.
"This is how I want you," he says to me.
When I don't want to please him, his barbaric hands reach me,
and I hate him but need him to love me.
The stones of my house are carved
with dampened dreams, pale caresses,
and distorted figures that follow me.
I already speak like him.
I even think like him sometimes,
yet burning my house would be useless.
My temple would remain standing,
and if I destroy it, the dust and particles would scatter in air
already contaminated; they would fly aimlessly without rest,
without shelter, and shivers would be felt throughout
as a result of another wandering ghost without a name.

Name

I want a name of wonder and lust
that provokes the tongue
and sticks to the ear,
a name with waltz and jazz,
romance and sass,
cherry seeds and lemon peels.
I need a powerful name,
bruised and awoken
from many deaths,
a name that breaks free
and knows how to scream
when its essence is questioned.
I want a name unlike any other—
earth-shattering, mouth-watering,
wrapped in lavender, abundant in love,
a name that is mine and only I can create.

Beyond

I wanted to be painted as a dark-skinned goddess
with hair as dark as a raven's plumage,
a guitar-shaped waist with the flexibility of a serpent,
small bosom perfectly standing, strong thighs,
and longer legs with no stretch marks.
I wanted her to look like me, but not be me.
I wanted to be painted with eyes less droopy, alert and almost happy,
with a mysterious smile that hides the space
between my two bottom teeth—
nude with soft skin, erotic without seeming promiscuous.
I wanted to be surrounded by white camellias
or perhaps surrounded by nothing.
Between the void, I'd be the light,
but he painted me fragmented—
with cubes even on my buttocks—
holding a guitar that covered my sunflower.
My eyes were drawn to her angular face,
a face with blurry corners, lips of disappearing strawberries,
and eyes closed or almost opened—
meditative, peaceful, perhaps disheartened.
Oh, the heart offered with all its trinkets and treasures,
rancors and pleasures—
to be unraveled or misunderstood—
and then, like a kiss, it came to me:
the artist, in his moment of inspiration, captured what I couldn't see.

Cindy

My uncle's friend had pictures of girls hidden
under his mattress. He even had one of
my sister Michelle and cousin Tammy.
I was only eleven or twelve when he went to jail for touching—
not my sister or cousin, but other girls.
Michelle and Tammy grew up to be even
more beautiful. I, however, was always a different seed.
I didn't look like my mom and was the ill-favored version
of my dad, who'd tell me a little makeup
would go a long way. I learned the art of covering.
I'm a waning crescent moon forced to come out
when she doesn't want to. During showers, I try
to keep my eyes closed as I make myself clean—
as I feel my body. I swear I didn't want to be
touched at eleven or twelve; I wanted to be liked,
yet I was never a desire in anyone's dreams or perversions.
Marriage is an illusion for me, so I've stopped
searching for a man. I need an artist to paint me as he sees me,
for he can find beauty in ugly things.

Michelle's Secret

I heard mornings are tough for you;
you wake up sad and crying.
I heard mornings are tough for you;
you wake up sad and crying.
You feel worthless and dirty,
and you wanna give up trying.

It doesn't matter if the sun's out
because the torment's got you down.
It doesn't matter if the sun's out
because the torment's got you down.
You try to keep it together;
you smile when going about town.

The evil man hurt you so much,
and you often feel ashamed.
The evil man hurt you so much,
and you often feel ashamed.
But it wasn't your clothes or fault,
Sara; you shouldn't take the blame.

It happened to my friend too;
her pain she tries not to show.
It happened to my friend too;
her pain she tries not to show.
She was touched by her uncle's friend,
and her family doesn't know.

Remains

While sleeping, I saw my grandmother,
in a white nightgown, asking for air—
a tired angel, but with radiant skin, hidden wrinkles,
and stains, covered in dye.
She knew how to read the lines on the palm of her hand.
She knew what was coming. She knew it was close,
the day that her nightmare of fallen teeth would gain life,
and she'd have to chew them and taste all the
unpleasantness of the past:
three times raped,
three dead children.
She'd have to experiment the thirst of uncertainty,
the doubt, the worst of the abysses,
and the guilt of doubting what was lived.
She must have heard the crow sing thrice.
The sun awoke, and there she lay still—
with eyes opened from fear or astonishment,
without teeth, a smile, or tears—
wearing a hospital nightgown that smelled like
sweat and wilted flowers.
I left a white rose on her tomb,
and in my moments of doubt, I convince myself
that such a pure soul could never cease to be.

**To The Saxophone Abuela Bought For My Aunt
Who Later Passed It On To My Mother,
Who Handed It To Me…**

If I knew how to write an ode, I would write one to the
saxophone I used to play in my youth.
I would write it in pen and include
the smudges and crossed-out words.
I would write it near a window at five o'clock in the morning,
the same time Abuela would wake up to say her prayers.
I would establish a pattern or rhythm and perhaps
begin it with a statement identifying myself,
not a question like "Do you remember me from high school?"
but something much more profound.
I would express my gratitude for jazz and swing,
improvisation and freedom, risks and candor, passion and heart.
I would confess how its tone color and language
have taken my breath away and illuminated my path.

My beloved instrument is worthy of an ode
both flowery and rugged, and if I could,
I would write one with conviction and remorse.
I would offer an apology for my neglect.
~~I wouldn't mention our disagreements~~
~~or complain about its squeaking.~~
~~I wouldn't try to explain that~~
I let everything go because I was a little lazy
and felt inadequate. My heart has been off beat.
There are so many feelings I wish to release.
I wish I could explain that I wasn't disenchanted
by its old age or the dent in its bell.
I didn't want to change it. I didn't wanna repair it,
for the dent was evidence of struggle and hard work,
and Abuela knew it would mark us forever.

Ave María, if I could only write an ode, I would
remind my esteemed saxophone how it was chosen—
how Abuela saved money from her three jobs to give us music
so we could create our own.
I would propose a new beginning.
I would end it with what I've learned:
sacrifice and perseverance bear much fruit,
and deep-rooted love guides you to growth.

Fear

Her hair carried ash;
her eyes, not windows,
but cobblestones,
weighed down my skin,
pinched my nerves—
I turned cold.
My spine curved
as she gave my brother
a glass of dirty water.
He drank it,
for it was far better than thirst.
She then carved with her fingernails
our wooden table,
with her sinister smile
engendered an eclipse.
And everyone continued eating,
though they felt her presence there,
because they couldn't see her.
They could only taste the gradual decay.

Mind-full

I close my eyes.
I see butterflies and swans,
sunsets of violet and blue.
I try not to stay sad for too long;
I'm no longer a child stuck
in a house with no music or books.
I see seashells on a beach,
like the one I went to when
I was twenty. I see the sandcastle I couldn't build.
I close my eyes and see my mother crying;
Father hits her hard. I open my eyes. I wipe them dry.
I close them again. I'm back at the beach. I listen to
the sounds of a shell. I breathe into it—return it to the waters,
and it always comes back as a nightmare or a dream.

A Dream

She was making rice and stirring a pot of *pollo guisao*
beautifully, meticulously, *cariñosamente*.
I contemplated her.
"Smells good, right, *mija*?"
A plethora of flowers fell from the heavens—
magenta, purple, blue, and silver.
They descended gracefully,
 le lo lai   le lo le lo lai,
carrying me to a fertile land.
I saw a *jibarito* delighting in the freshly cut grass.
With a melody on his lips and *yerbas* in his tattered hands,
he scattered the seeds with care—
magia.
Mamí continued mixing-
a sprinkling of water on my head,
warm, therapeutic, *relajante*.
I closed my eyes, releasing all weariness,
but my peace was interrupted.
She stopped stirring,
and I awoke to an empty stove:
no *pollo guisao*, no flowers, no song.

The Question

It's not just stories:
The flying cat saving the baby elephant trapped in a well
or the cocoa dust easing pain when the funny bone is hit or
the pinky toe stubbed.
The tree branches give hugs;
the leaves rustle a lullaby
that cradles the fear of
having no stardust, lightning bugs, or torn cocoons.
The melody resounds in sleep,
follows in dreams,
accompanies dinners,
provoking laughter
while a piece of steak or chicken is being chewed—
tucked within
until it's finally released,
as it was for me
that once upon a time
on a night of a crescent moon:
"Tell me, Grandpa—how does an oyster give birth to a pearl?"

The Door

Ana covers the gap beneath
with handkerchiefs and rags.
She stares at it several times,
turns the knob
left, right,
right, left—
pulls it,
goes to bed,
wakes up in an hour
to do the same
because he could come in while she sleeps.
She has nightmares of it:
he covers her lips,
ties her legs,
presses her belly.
She tries to avoid his gaze,
but her eyes are held wide open for the
morphing of the young man into her grandmother
wearing a cream colored robe:
"Remember the garden with the cement path?
How you skipped through it to grab a blue orchid?"
Ana's body is lifted;
below she sees a little girl with a bloody knee
and her grandmother's teeth in her hands.
"I should've been more careful," the little girl cries.
Ana's body drops like rain splattering the ground.
She feels her chest tightening,
her words being wiped away with an old, pungent cloth.
Her grandmother grips her neck.
Ana does not beg
but observes her dwelling:
the plastic covered sofa,
the piles of clothes on the living room floor,
and her shoes next to the locked door.

Guilt

From spoils, I've built my house.
I keep my windows closed
and the blinds shut. I check the stove,
the door, and all the plugs many times before bed.
I wake up from nightmares and check them
once or twice more.
I can't let an intruder find me.
I can't let my house be consumed by flames
though I myself am burning.
I want to be good seed.
I want to be made clean.
I don't want bad things happening
because of my fault.

Iker

Uncle Iker was banished, I heard,
for biting a mouse until its guts
squirted on his face and ground,
and he became sick with worms,
and then strong, not like a mouse,
but an unearthly creature,
quick, cunning, and conniving—
with eyes that made one wonder
about the possibility of redemption
moments before being consumed.

Daughter

In my dream,
I was a doll
on a revolving pedestal—
a doll with long, black hair,
wearing a white dress
that sparkled like Father's
cold, blue eyes.
He taught us how to see the world,
a space of suffering
with few pockets of joy—
with people who love you for a moment
and then discard you
after you've fulfilled a purpose.

In my dream, people loved me.
I was beautiful.
My smile was a sunrise,
reflecting only what I wanted to show.

Father was good.
He worked overtime.
Father was bad.
He beat us with belt buckles and pulled our hair.
Father was good.
He beat us because he wanted to protect us.
Mother told on us.
Mother was bad.
She knew it would get him angry,
but she wanted him to love her.

In my dream, no one saw me cry.
Father hated crying. He said it shows weakness,
so he got mad instead. Mother cried all the time:
when Father came late,
when he called her ugly,
when he hit her for looking at a man's chest on TV.

It was all for our own good, Father told us.
His momma never beat him.
His daddy never beat him.
They gave him away.
They let him go.

Blue notes to wash the soil.
Blue notes to gather the soil.
Blue notes to part the sea.

I'm looking for a lullaby that can help me fall asleep—
a blue light, a blue dream.
In my dream, I was lonely, as I am now,
standing on a rotating pedestal,
smiling before an audience,
crying when my back was turned.

Sorry—

it's not that I didn't forgive you.
It's that your sins are shadows,
spider webs, shriveled sunflowers,
the creak of an empty rocking chair,
a stream of dissonant notes,
an unwanted accompaniment,
a tear in the tablecloth,
the stitches on an old shirt,
a candle on top of a mantel
with a feeble flame that never dies,
a dusty, blue lampshade on
a glass table needing daily cleaning—
sometimes more than once—
a cluttered corner,
a carved tree,
a chipped sapphire,
a lined piece of paper
with eraser marks and smudges
because remembering and reconstructing
swing on a pendulum;
they form crossroads,
leaving you wondering
whether you'll be able to trust again.

Frescavena y Morir Soñando*

"I'm going to teach you about malice," he said—
because people carry evil in their hearts,
and pity only kills,
unexpectedly, like
an infirmity you feed
until it curtails your exuberance,
and the possibility of renewal is
as distant as a blood moon.
My mother's bloody lip didn't bother;
my sister's black eye gave me the acuity of an eagle.
Love is woe.
It comes in the shape of a belt buckle,
a phone receiver,
a spiked heel.
Words fly in overcast skies.
An "I love you" is a feather, a flower petal,
or a clock in distress,
falling back, sprinting forward.
The questions are When? and How?
They taunt you in the shower,
slice your wrists,
whisper, "Soon…You shall see."
A taciturn, shriveled spirit in oversized clothing,
awaiting a new song to awaken it,
but instead hears the tune once recorded
in a little machine,
a melody about ice cream and sprinkles,
spaceships and galaxies,
butterflies and daisies.
Can the flower petals be put together?
Can I catch the words,
scramble and unscramble them—
change the letters,
the diction,
the intonation?

Can I convert them into sugar cubes,
float on them to prevent me from drowning in a glass of water?
Can I eradicate the phrases invaded by exclamation points?
"You're going to learn!"
"This is so you won't ever forget!"
I didn't.
Some things are ephemeral.
Others remain caught in the edges and corners of a bathtub.

I scraped the residue with my fingernails,
tucked it under my doormat,
and every so often,
I crawl to it
because stepping on it with solely my feet
isn't good enough.

**Frescavena* and *morir soñando* are popular Hispanic beverages. The former is translated as "fresh oats," and the latter means "to die dreaming."

Liberation

I killed her.
Her screams echoed as she descended into oblivion,
flailing her arms with intense horror,
as if she were trying to hold onto something,
but you can't hold onto air.
I'm bewildered by her look of disbelief—
did she not know?
She pushed me off the precipice—
I threw her out the window,
dragged her out of her chair
where she sat gorging on toast and jelly.
I choked her, punched her, scratched her face
for sticking her claws into my lover's heart.
She faded into the distance.
My heart and head pounded...
Haunted by her shrieks—
her body on the pavement.
What have I done?
A fallen angel cast out of the kingdom,
condemned to live in darkness,
I picked up the knife
glistening on the table
and thrust it into my stomach.
My cries permeated the room like the weeping woman
attempting to scavenge her children from the river.
    I woke up screeching and
        frantically ran towards the slightly opened window,
        allowing the crisp air to caress my face,
        exhaling puffy clouds in the shape of small dragons.

Speak

Shameful, sterile Silence,
will you rip out your tongue?
You've heard the ringing in your ears.
You've seen the dimming sunset.
You've felt the weeping in the wind,

yet you reverently scour the
white patches on your tongue.
The patches return, and you,
Silence, stem of trepidation
curled up in a smoke-filled room,
adjust and overlook
the spoiled berries, the arid soil,
the anemic butterflies on the ground.

You don't step on them.
You convince yourself of your rectitude.
You didn't cause the fall.
You let them be.
You let them become and decompose
into the patches of your fruitless bite.

Stay Silent

It takes four generations to break a curse.
Mother told Sister she won't have kids
because she's bad seed. Poor Sister lost five:
four miscarriages and
one stillborn—stay still spell
bred by her giver who begat it from her maker
who got it from his creator.
                    Push.   Push the jinx away.
Sister prayed. Mother thought her prayers
were no good 'cause they were either
too soggy or too stale and missing
some grit and bone, and flowers ain't gonna grow:
"She needs to pray harder. She needs to push more."
"But she's got a sincere heart, Momma."
                    Push.   Push the jinx away.
Mother said Sister's got a dirty heart, and
she needs to make herself good:
"Drink these soapy suds, cleanse your tongue,
purify your insides."
"That's gonna make her sick, Momma."
                    Push.   Push the jinx away.
Sister pushed stillborn baby.
Baby never cried.
Sister often cries.
Therapist told her to meditate.
She meditates in her cage for four
minutes and thirty-three seconds.
She's got the faith of a mustard seed
and the hatred of a mountain.

Accent

It's my melody.
I will not get rid of it.
Do you understand?

Omnipresent: An Ode to My Accent

And so often, it is said, "Words cannot express what I'm feeling,"
but you, my esteemed and beloved accent,
know the intricacies of my tongue, the vibrations
of my vocal chords, the arpeggios in my throat.
My Wholehearted Arranger,
Passionate Conductor,
Devoted Accompanist,
you understand every note in my laments, hymns, and melodies.
I elevate your name, for you are worthy of dignity,
praise, and recognition.
It is because of you that my voice has acquired such tone color.
You taught me how to blend flavors, intertwine stories of
my bloodline, how to see beyond the sun.
You have shown me how to savor every syllable, nuance, and sound.
O great master of music, inclusive and inviting,
don't you ever be frightened. Don't you ever hush.
I am beholden to your unswerving love. I crown you with flowers.
I'll defend your honor, for I have found
the beauty in my voice. You are a treasure,
a masterpiece produced by years of
struggle, triumphs, and survival. I am delighted to be your vessel.
There won't be a wall between us. I will not get rid of you.

Duende

I guzzle the words,
swallow each note, as if they were marshmallows
made out of the moon.
I breathe in the air,
the moisture and dryness—
take in the pollen, the lavender,
the rain and thunder,
till I weaken,
and my senses heighten.
It's more than skin crawling and hair rising.
I am elevated beyond perspective—
where a cascade begins, where it ends,
inside a cocoon, between the sun's rays.
A transformative, timeless pilgrimage:
I, with two heads, enter a cave,
play with skulls, and dance with souls.
I'm not afraid of tomorrow.
The melody of a quena ushers me out.
I am an Andean condor stretching its wings.

Hope

Worthless. Robbed of opportunities, security, and peace.
Unlucky. A stranger to fortune.
I've tried—oh, how hard I've tried to gather my lost belongings,
but they won't return.
Empty—
like a musical jewelry box waiting to store new pearls,
the most marvelous of all pearls, yet it can happen
because there's more than enough room

for unforeseen treasures.

Vidal

I gave him three cups of water despite being
told to give only one. It was the first time
I beheld his face. I saw half-eaten yams,
trees, and ruins in his big, brown eyes.
His smile was a crescent moon
whose light dimmed

when

the surrounding noise
spoiled the crops, cut the trunks,
and removed the stones and pillars.

The next day, and a few times after that,
I went looking for him at the corner
where he would sit with his guitar
and empty tangerine can.
Oh, how I hoped he had found a dwelling so
he could greet his guests at the door,
offer them something to drink, and
play pieces of a landscape.

I cried without crying.
I prayed without kneeling
to see those eyes again
until three to four weeks later

when

I saw him once more:
He gave me a silver brooch
in a clear plastic sandwich bag.
It was missing a sapphire gemstone
on one of its flower petals.

Beyond Perspective

Where cascades begin,
inside cocoons, between rays,
I find the answers.

Perspectives

I saw a seahorse giving birth.
He saw lightning bugs coming
out of a saxophone.
"How do you not see the miracle of life?" I asked,
and thus, he responded with a question:
"How do you not gaze upon the wonder that is music?"
We stood in front of the abstract painting,
admiring the use of pink, green, lavender,
and different kinds of blue.
I drowned in its power.
I held on to the waters, the coral reefs, and the seagrass.
He was enveloped by its pulse, the melismas, and the blue notes.
Sempre più. More water. More rebirth.
We discussed it during dinner and right before bed.
We were moved. We were full. We were rich from
the pearl we discovered.

BEYOND

I found the answers
when the sky was
layered in pink, lavender,
and celestial blue.
I am a medicine woman
though my breasts have
never produced milk, and
my womb is barren.
I'm not bad seed.
My name has a face comprised
of geometrical shapes and eighth notes.
I am whole. I delight in the taste
of strawberries before I slumber.
The sweetness makes up a moon,
and I dream of incredible things
that I can make happen despite
being worn down by distorted
figures and dismissed by pale caresses.
My body heals.
Our bodies heal
on their own
with the help of others—
with the love from BEYOND.

Elaine Nadal is a writer and educator. She holds a master's degree in liberal studies from Wesleyan University, as well as degrees in Spanish secondary education and fine arts (music). She enjoys translating and traveling and has studied in Spain and Puerto Rico. A Pushcart and Best of the Net nominee, she has been published in several journals, including *Pilgrimage Magazine, Haight Ashbury Literary Journal, Shemom, Antarctica Journal, Red River Review, Rigorous Magazine, Arsenic Lobster, Grasslimb, La Casita Grande Lounge, Flypaper Magazine, Autumn Sky Poetry Daily, Hoot Review, The Write Launch, Latino Book Review Magazine,* and *Haunted Waters Press.* Her first poetry chapbook *Sweat, Dance, Sing, Cut.* was published by Finishing Line Press in 2019. Elaine has produced and appeared on several episodes of Valley Shore Community Television's *Poetry of Immigrants.* For her, writing is a way of making sofrito out of the experiences and varied truths of life. It is also a way of honoring the memory of her Abuela Flor, from whom she learned about struggle, determination, compassion, and love.

www.ingramcontent.com/pod-product-compliance
Lightning Source LLC
LaVergne TN
LVHW041510070426
835507LV00012B/1458